ISBN 978-0-428-15792-0
PIBN 11255288

1 MONTH OF
FREE
READING

at

www.ForgottenBooks.com

By purchasing this book you are eligible for one month membership to ForgottenBooks.com, giving you unlimited access to our entire collection of over 1,000,000 titles via our web site and mobile apps.

To claim your free month visit:

www.forgottenbooks.com/free1255288

English
Français
Deutsche
Italiano
Español
Português

www.forgottenbooks.com

Mythology Photography **Fiction**
Fishing Christianity **Art** Cooking
Essays Buddhism Freemasonry
Medicine **Biology** Music **Ancient
Egypt** Evolution Carpentry Physics
Dance Geology **Mathematics** Fitness
Shakespeare **Folklore** Yoga Marketing
Confidence Immortality Biographies
Poetry **Psychology** Witchcraft
Electronics Chemistry History **Law**
Accounting **Philosophy** Anthropology
Alchemy Drama Quantum Mechanics
Atheism Sexual Health **Ancient History**
Entrepreneurship Languages Sport
Paleontology Needlework Islam
Metaphysics Investment Archaeology
Parenting Statistics Criminology
Motivational

Historic, Archive Document

Do not assume content reflects current
scientific knowledge, policies, or practices.

uction

Even though there has been tremendous support for this
newsletter, the length maybe a problem for some individuals.
The entire newsletter is not meant to be read by everyone.
The headings are intended to lead you to information of value
to you. The same type information is included in this in this
newsletter as in previous editions.

nza

It may not be time to panic, but healthy concern would
certainly be in order. Several confirmed cases of H5N2
have occured in Pennsylavania, New Jersey, or Massachusetts.
Various state personnel are optimistic and are in charge of
the situation at this time. For more information, contact the
Pennsylvania Department of Agriculture Hotline
(1-800-932-0904) or the Pennsylvania Poultry Federation at
(717-652-7530). Personnel in affected states may also
contact their respection Department of Agriculture. See
enclosure.

Remember
Beware of live bird markets and small flocks. Crates and
other equipment of contract haulers or others traveling
between companies must be cleaned and disinfected after each
use, and all should be. Sell all birds in the flock. Follow
biosecurity procedures.

tion

The address we provided in the last newsletter for the
National Turkey Federation was wrong.
Delete: Reston International Center
         Suite 302
         Zip 22091
Insert: 11319 Sunset Hills Road
         Zip 22090

unities

1) New York –
The Department of Poultry and Avian Sciences at Cornell
University, have announced the opening of a position as
Extension Associate in Poultry Science. Application deadline
is March 14, 1986, with the date available being

April 1, 1986. They prefer a Ph.D, with an M.S. required, in Poultry or Animal Sciences. The salary is commensurate with qualifications and experience. They are interested in someone to develop and coordinate a statewide Extension program involving youth and small flock activities. For more information contact:

  Dr. Dan L. Cunningham
  Department of Poultry and Avian Sciences
  Cornell University
  204 Rice Hall
  Ithaca, NY 14853
  607-256-3168

2) Hawaii
A position as an Assistant or Associate Specialist in Poultry is now available at the University of Hawaii at Manoa. The closing date is May 1, 1986 or until a suitable candidate is identified. The duties include - to provide leadership, direction and assistance in the development of their poultry Extension program, teach an undergraduate poultry production course; opportunity to participate in departmental research. Salary ranges are $25,320-37,488 for the Assistant, and $32,040-47,436 for the Associate level, with 4-years post Ph.D experience required for the Associate level. For more information contact:

  Dr. Charles W. Weems, Chairman
  Department of Animal Sciences
  University of Hawaii
  1800 East-West Road
  Honalulu, HI 96822
  808-948-8295

Story 1) Bill Merka, University of Georgia, recently made a two day trip to Washington to visit with personnel in Agricultural Marketing Services (AMS), Food Safety and Inspection Service (FSIS), and other agencies. The purposes were to: 1) obtain answers to specific poultry processing questions; and 2) Introductory - to establish a rapport with these personnel. Bill used my office as his base. He reported this was a very beneficial trip and he intends to come back as needed to work on specific programs or problems. I would like to again extend this invitation to any of you to use my office area as needed, and to meet with personnel in Extension or other agencies.

  2) The University of Georgia Poultry Science Department had a booth at the Southeastern Poultry and Egg Association Trade Show. Part of the booth display was devoted to recruiting material used by the department. A leaflet described the University of Georgia campus, the department, course, and personnel. This is one example of what a department can do in the area of recruiting students.

3) Virginia Tech is sponsoring the Twentieth Annual Poultry
Processors Workshop, to be held March 5, 1986. This is a
one day meeting, having topics that include - USDA updates by
AMS and FSIS personnel; Quality Control ; and the impact of
the Residue Avoidance Program. Due to logistics,
scheduling, or money problems, most companies cannot afford
to send personnel in many management positions to regional
workshops (e.g. those sponsored by Southeastern). To be most
value to the company, personnel need to be kept current, and
be rewarded at least occasionally with trips to meetings.
The cost of educational opportunities such as this can easily
be justified by employee morale, and the savings generated by
just one idea. Meetings such as this successfully, meet the
need of updating a greater cross section of personnel than is
normally possible.

4) The North American Gamebird Association held the annual
meeting in Bilox, Mississippi January 15-19. The meeting
consisted of educational workshops, instruction in necropsy
and equipment displays. The meeting was very successful, with
record attendence. Those interested in working with the gamebird industry should consider attending the next meeting in
New Orleans, and becoming a member of this professional
organization. For more information contact:
       John Mullin, Executive Director
       North American Gamebird Assn., Inc.
       Rt. 1 Box 96 - Wildlife Harvest
       Goose Lake, Iowa 52750

5) Pennsylvania Game Bird Conference - The Poultry Science
Department at The Pennsylvania State University has announced
that the Game Bird Production and Management of Shooting
Preserves annual conference will be held Febrary 24-25, 1986.
The course is designed for anyone interested in game birds or
hunting resort operation. It has sessions designed primarily
for experienced producers, but would be beneficial for
beginners. The conference is normally attended by 100
producers from eight states and has enjoyed many years of
success. For more information, contact Herb Jordan.

The following information is provided for those Extension
n   specialists having an interest in working with the gamebird
d   industry. Licensed game farms, meat bird facilities,
Inc.   and hunting preserves are no longer just an interesting
hobby, or even a way of life - they have enolved into a
growing, challenging business. The North American Gamebird
Association, Inc. (like other trade associations) is a non-
profit organization of business competitors who work together
to solve mutal problems and improve net income. The purpose
of NAGA is to promote, protect and improve the gamebird
breeding and hunting preserve industries. The individuals
and program participants at NAGA conventions come from
diverse backgrounds--state game departments, industry,

members of the Association, related professions,universities,
etc. The Association encourages its members to follow the
Code of Ethics which protect them from unscrupulous business
practices, and discourages government intervention. They
promote fair and honest dealings, the sale of sound birds and
hatching eggs, true representation of our stock ,courteous
and prompt service to the customer, cooperation with our
customers to insure their success, and adherence to fair
trade practices. The membership fee includes 12 issues of
Wildlife Harvest, (50-60 pages, edited by John Mullin) a
yearly Directory of all NAGA members, and information
sources. For more information, contact:

> Walter S. Walker, Secretary
> P.O. Box 2105
> Cayce-West Columbia, SC 29171
> 803-796-8163

1
le

1) New Agricultural Yearbook -
The New Agricultural Yearbook analyzes how American
agriculture interacts with the Nation's economy, how it
functions in the international trade area, and how it is
affected by apparently unrelated domestic polices. Copies
may be available from individual Congressmen. Single copies
can be available from the Superintendent of Documents,
Government Printing Office, Washington, D.C 20402 for $10.00.

2) 1982 Census of Agriculture -
Information from the 1982 Census of Agriculture, including
state and national summary data (no charge for a printed
copy), is now available from the Public Information Office of
the U.S. Bureau of the Census, Washington, D.C. 20233.
Telephone 301-763-4040. Contact Steve Stanley, Public
Information Officer, Agriculture Division, at the address
above for multiple copies of the kit. Stanley also has an
excellent 12-minute slide-tape presentation on the 1982
Census of Agriculture available by request. A graphic
summary of this data cost $9.50; GPO stock No.003-024-06362-0.

3) National Poultry Improvement Plan (NPIP) -
The NPIP is a voluntary program for the blood testing and
certication of Poultry breeding flocks for certain egg-
transmitted, hatchery- disseminated diseases. The staff of
NPIP will soon have available their annual directories of
participants for 1986. These directories are published in
two volumes and list the name and address of the participant,
the hatching egg capacity of the hatchery, the stock handled,
and the disease control programs for which their products are
certified. Also available is a publication listing, by
States, the number of participating flocks, the number of
breeders tested for each disease program, the number of
positive flocks, and the size of the average breeding flock
in the program. Similar participation data are provided
concerning the hatcheries, dealers, and independents
breeding flocks. These publications are:

APHIS 91-41 - 1986 Directory of Participants Handling Egg -
           Type and Meat-Type Chickens and Turkeys
APHIS 91-42 - 1986 Directory of Participants Handling Water-
           fowl, Exhibition Poultry, and Gamebirds
APHIS 91-43 - Table of Hatchery and Flock Participation
           1983-84 and 1984-85
To order copies, contact:
      NPIP
      USDA/APHIS Veterinary Service
      Room 828, Federal Center Building #1
      Hyattsville, MD   20782

4) Gamebird Resource Lists -
   a) The 1985 Missouri Gamebird Directory has recently
      been printed. To obtain a copy contact Glenn
      Geiger, who prepared this publication.
   b) A Resource List for Gamebird Producers, Fanciers, and
      other Poultry Producers, General Report #112, has been
      prepared by Richard Reynnells. Contact Chuck Strong
      at the University of Georgia for a copy.

5) Animal Health Data Base -
The new electronic data base "Animal Health Information
Service" available through the USDA Online menu on the ITT
Dialcom System is a pilot project of several USDA Agencies
(CSRS, APHIS, ES), and the Food and Drug Administration. It
began October 1, 1985. The information often is not
available in "hard copy" (printed form), but only from a
computer data base.
Source: Extension Service Update, Agricultural Programs
January-February 1986.

6) Science Workbook Available -
"The Science Workbook of Student Research Projects in Food
Agriculture - National Resources", 1985 edition; edited by
Dr. Edward E. Darrow is now available. This Workbook is
intended to be a handbook for high school and middle school
Science teachers and students. Most authors have written
their projects and articles with student readers as their
target audience. The projects in this book can be used as
demonstrations in the laboratory or classroom to help the
teacher illustrate the practical application of basic science
principles. Or, this workbook can serve as a resource from
which students can select topics for independent investi-
gation to present at science fairs. Also, you may find ideas
for 4-H or other youth projects. The project vary in level of
difficulty to accomodate both the gifted and average student.
Topic headings include: Conducting a Research Project: For
the Young Scientist; Animal Nutrition; Animal Physiology and
Biochemistry; Animal Reproduction;; Food Science and Food
Products; Insects; Plant Physiology and Biochemistry; Soil
Biology; and Guidelines for Animal Use. One copy of this 109
page workbook will be provided at no charge. For more

information, contact:
- Dr. Edward E. Darrow
  College of Agriculture
  The Ohio State University
  2120 Fyffe Rd.
  Columbus, OH 43210
  614-422-1734

7) Anatomy Reprints available to Library -
Dr. Alfred Lucas through his many years in research has acquired a large volume of one-of-a-kind reprints of anatomy articles. These reprints cover all aspects of the anatomy of Aves and other zoological classifications. We would like these reprints to be included in a university library so they may be readily available for reference. If you are interested in obtaining the following material for your work in poultry, contact me, or Dr. Cal Flegal or Dr. Lucas at Michigan State University.
1) Ten 4-drawer file cabinets and about 8 egg cases of reprints; several translated articles; indexed.
2) There is also a large amount of blood slides of wild birds classified by order, family, genus, species; and other tissue or blood slides.
3) There is other anatomy equipment and drawings; also copper or lead plates for the unfinished Avian Anatomy Vol. 2, by Chamberlain.

I included this section for those interested in knowing more about the successes of the poultry industry, and how this information is being preserved. In January 1952, at the Boston Poultry Show a few people met informally and selected Herb Alp to head an organization committee. In June of 1952, this committee met in New York City, and the American Poultry Historical Society was organized. At the annual meeting in 1953 plans were developed for a Poultry Hall of Fame. From 1954 to 1970 portraits of honorees were displayed in Jull Hall, University of Maryland. In 1970, the Poultry Hall of Fame was moved to the National Agricultural Library at Beltsville, Maryland. The purpose of the American Poultry Historical Society is to find, collect, and preserve records, pictures, materials and objects connected with the development of the Poultry Industry of America, and to make available its great history to this and future generations and to honor or recognize persons for outstanding achievement or leadership in the industry. In 1974 the Society published the book "American PoultryHistory", 1823-1973. This 775 page volume was the most complete coverage of the history of any food animal species. Copies are still available from the society. Persons interested in membership or further information should contact American Poultry Historical Society, c/o Poultry Science Department, 1675 Observatory Dr., Room 260, University of Wisconsin, Madison, WI 53706

Avian Anatomy Volume Sent	You may have wondered why you received some volumes of Avian Anatomy, Integument, Volumes 1 and 2. Storage space has been at a premium at USDA and some, if not all, of these volumes were to be discarded. Personnel at NPIP have sent or will send volumes to Extension personnel based on my estimates of need; or in response to specific requests. Volumes in excess of requirements can be saved for future students or a set given to your university library. There are a few sets left at Michigan State and I have a few sets in this office. If you need more, call or write and they will be sent first come, first serve.
From the Federal Register	1) Importation of Poultry Hatching Eggs. The Animal and Plant Health Inspection Service (APHIS) has announced a 60-day extension of the comment period for the proposed rule that would amend the import regulations for poultry hatching eggs. This topic was covered in this newsletter, Vol. 1, No. 7. Briefly, they would 1) delete the quarantine requirement for hatching eggs from VVND free countries; and; 2) clarify the quarantine period of hatching eggs and poultry from these eggs. Written comments must be received on or before March 7, 1986. Refer to Docket No. 82-107 when making comments. As stated previously submit written comments to:

     Thomas O. Gessel, Director
     Regulatory Coordination Staff
     APHIS/USDA   Room 728
     Federal Building
     6505 Belcrest Road
     Hyattsville, MD 20782

For further information, contact:
     Dr. S.S. Richardson, Chief Staff Veterinarian
     Import/Export Animals and Products Staff
     VS, APHIS, USDA   Room 843
     Federal Building
     6505 Belcrest Road
     Hyattsville, MD 20782
     301-436-8172

Source: Federal Register, Vol. 51, No. 4; Tuesday, January 7, 1986,   page 613.

2) Money –
The Cooperative State Research Service (CSRS) has announced that applications are invited for competitive grant awards under the Special Reserch Grants Program, for fiscal year 1986. The Secretary may award grants for period not to exceed five years for the support of research projects to further the following program areas applicable to poultry: 1) respiratory disease; 2) metabolic and immunologic diseases; 3) enteric disorders. Research should be directed toward: 1) basic studies to clarify disease problems; or 2) develop- ment of practical management systems that prevent or alleviate

animal losses. To be considered for funding during fiscal
year 1986 proposals must be received by March 10, 1986.
Copies of the "Research Grant Application Kit", more
information, and Administrative Provisions governing the
program may be obtained by contacting:
    Grants Administrative Management
    Attn: Proposal Services Unit
    Office of Grants and Program Systems
    USDA Room 007 J.S. Morrill Building
    15th & Independence Ave., S.W.
    Washington, DC 20251
    202-475-5049
Source: Federal Register, Vol 50, No. 245; Friday,
December 20, 1985, page 52204-52206.

3) Streamlined Inspection Service (SIS) -
The Food Safety and Inspection Service (FSIS) is requesting
comments regarding an interim rule that amends the
Federal poultry inspection regulations to establish the SIS
method of inspection. The new system is to be implemented
in establishments now operating under Modified Traditional
Inspection (MTI). SIS in corporates new procedures that
require one or two inspectors and a Finished Product Standards
(FPS) program for evaluating the wholesomeness and
acceptability of the finsihed product. The traditional, MTI,
New Line Speed (NELS) and SIS systems are described in this
Federal Register article. They also include definitions of
nonconformance, and finished product standards in a table
format. The program is effective January 29,1986, and
comments must be received on or before March 31, 1986.
Address written comments to:
    USDA
    FSIS, Policy Office
    Attn: Hearing Clerk
    Room 3803 South Bldg.
    Washinton, DC 20250
For further information, or to make oral comments, contact :
    Dr. Douglas L. Berndt, Director
    Slaughter Inspection Standards & Procedures Division
    Meat & Poultry Inspection Technical Service
    FSIS/USDA
    Washington, DC 20250
    202-447-3219
Source: Federal Register; Vol. 51, No. 19; Wednesday,
January 29,1986   page 3569-3580.

4) Facility and Equipment Requirements for SIS. FSIS is
proposing to establish facility and equipment requirements
for establishments operating under the SIS for broilers and
cornish game hens. The changes would specify dimensions of
the inspection and reinspection stations for SIS. These
changes include the installation of an appropriately
designed, adjustable platform at each inspector's
station, and would require a carcass selection device
(selector, kickout) at inspection stations. The changes also

specify lighting, handwashing, and other equipment requirements. Docket No. 85-036P. Comments must be received on or before February 28, 1986. Written comments should be sent to:

Policy Office
Attn: Annie Johnson
FSIS Hearing Clerk
Room 3803 South Bldg.
USDA/FSIS
Washington, DC 20250

For further information or to provide oral comments contact:

Dr. Douglas L. Berndt, Director
Slaughter Inspection Standard & Procedures Division
Meat & Poultry Inspection Technical Services
USDA/FSIS
Washington, DC 20250
202-447-3219

National Agricultural Library (NAL)

The NAL, with a total collection of 1.8 million volumes, is one of the largest agricultural libraries in the world. It is the coordinator and primary resource for a national network of state land-grant and field libraries and serves agricultural libraries nationwide. The Library is the U.S. center for the international agricultural information system. Located on the grounds of the 7,000 acre Agricultural Research Center, in Beltsville, MD, it is one of three national libraries. The other are the Library of Congress and the National Libary of Medicine. The NAL offers many services, some of which are outlined here.

1) Biotechnology Information Center

The National Agricultural Library (NAL) announces the formation of a Biotechnology Information Center as part of a continuing effort to complement and support research priorities in U.S. agriculture. NAL is presently working to ensure that all relevant biotechnology literature is indexed and accessible worldwide through appropriate bibliographic services. One such service is AGRICOLA, the Libarary's computerized data base system and index to more than 2 million books and articles relating to all aspects of agriculture. Access to the AGRICOLA data base is possible through office and personal dial-up computer terminals, public or university libraries, and commercial search services. In attempting to track the literature of this increasingly and diverse discipline, NAL makes available to users several bibliographic aids which are international in scope. These include "Telegen Reporter" (file 238 on the DIALOG system) and "Derwent Abstracts" (file name "Biotech" on the Orbit System).

The Library through its Current Awareness Literature Service (CALS) keeps USDA personnel posted on recent literature published in the field of biotechnology. The CALS system searches Telegen, a data base of scientific, technical, and socioeconomic information related to genetic engineering and biotechnology drawn from 7,000 worldwide sources. Document delivery services based on resulting citations are provided

through NAL and the USDA Regional Document Delivery System.
NAL will also furnish to non-USDA users full-text documents
from the Telegen data base in either hardcopy or microfiche.
This service is available on a cost basis through the
Library's Lending Division. The Library is now meeting with
industry groups, Federal and State agencies and the scientific
community to identify sources of potential support for the
Information Center. For further information contact Jean
Bellows and/or Susan Whitmore, Biotechnology Information
Center Coordinator, NAL, Room 111, Beltsville,MD 20705,
301-344-3704.

2) Feed Composition Data Bank
The Feed Composition Data Bank (FCDB) is now operational
at the NAL. The data bank is one of the most complete
compilations of data on feedstuffs in the world, containg
information on more than 23,000 feeds. The NAL also offers
serveral FCDB publications which are available for purchase.
The FCDB relies heavily on current research for its nutrient
information collection activities. The Library actively
seeks any data contributions from researchers in the
feedstuffs community--government as well as industry.
The FCDB staff welcomes the opportunity to exchange feedstuffs information and disseminate feed composition tables.
For further information contact, the Feed Composition Data
Bank, Information Systems Division, NAL, Beltsville, MD 20705
301-344-3813

3) Food Irradation Information Center
The NAL has announced the formation of a national Food
Irradiation Information Center. This action is in response
to growing government and industry interest in the use of
radiation for food presentation and treatment. The NAL is
actively pursuing avenues of support for expansion in the
following areas:
Collection Development; Information Products; and Public
Services. For further information contact Carole Shore,
Food Irradiation Information Center Coordinator, National
Agricultural Library , Room 304, Beltsville, MD 20705;
301-344-4369.

4) Oral Histories and Archival Material
The Special Collections Program of the (NAL) welcomes the
opportunity to receive, preserve, and make available archival/
manuscript materials of historic value including diaries,
account books, letters, notebooks, memoirs, reminiscences, and
oral histories pertaining to agriculture and its many related
fields. The American Poultry Historical Society has been
cooperating in this project. Cititions to the interviews on
file may be accessed through AGRICOLA.
If you have an interest in pursuing this idea please contact
Dr. Alan Fusonie, Assistant Chief for Special Collections,
NAL, Beltsville, MD 20705; 301-344-3876.

5) Poultry Hall of Fame
The Poultry Hall Fame, housed in the reading room of the NAL
since 1972, has been relocated to NAL's second floor executive
offices. The special collection of portraiture recognizes
persons for outstanding achievement and leadership in the
poultry industry. The American Poultry Historical Society,

10

sponsors of the Poultry Hall of Fame, and the NAL have long cooperated to collect, disseminate, and preserve information about the development of the poultry industry in America. In 1971, the NAL received the James M. Gwin Poultry Collection of over 1,000 volumes--the personal working library of Dr. Gwin, a former professor of Poultry Husbandry and director of the Extension Service at the University of Marland. Complementing and supporting the Poultry Hall of Fame and the Gwin Collection at the NAL is one of the largest collections of poultry literature in the world, covering such subjects as anatomy, physiology, breeding, canning, diseases, equipment, feeding, hatcheries, marketing, processing, and statistics. National and worldwide access to NAL collections as well as future acquisitions will be available through AGRICOLA. For further information contact: Dr. Alan Fusonie, Special Collections, NAL, Room 301-A, Beltsville, MD 20705; 301-344-3876.

6) USDA Regional Document Delivery System (RDDS)
For approximately 11 years, land-grant university libraries have participated with the USDA, and the NAL, to provide documents and photocopies of articles to USDA personnel and libraries in the States and regions. The basic structure and operation of the RDDS are, briefly, as follows: USDA personnel and USDA field libraries in the states send their document requests to the major land-grant university library of that State. Requests are filled by the State land-grant library whenever possible with photocopies, microforms, or the loan of a hard copy volume sent directly to the requester. Requests not filled at the State land-grant library are then sent to the regional coordinating library, where they are filled if possible. Requests that remain unfilled at the regional level are then referred to the NAL for completion. Funding is accomplished by cooperative agreements between the regional coodinators and the NAL. For more information contact, John B. Forbes, Network Coordination, NAL, Room 204, Beltsville, MD 20705, (301) 344-1563. Copies of the full report for 1984 with comparative data for 1974-84 are available from the author.

Directory
Changes
1) Iowa - Change telephone numbers to:
    William Owings   515-294-4303
    Robert Hasiak   515-294-2572
    Jerry Sell   515-294-4002
    Darrell Trampel   515-294-0710
Note: For those new to Extension, Darrell is located at 2270
    Vet Medicine.
2) Mississippi -
Add: Robert W. Keirs, DVM
    College of Veterinary Medicine
    Poultry Pathology
    Drawer V
    Mississippi State University
    Mississippi State, MS 39762
    601-325-3432
    10% Extension

11

His areas of interest are reproductive efficiency and
pathology.
3) Rex Bushong has returned to Auburn as an Extension Poultry
Scientist. He will be responsible for general management and
nutrition of all poultry species. He has a 100% Extension
position. His address and telephone number are as listed in
your directory.
4) The supply of directories is nearly exhausted. Before
more copies are duplicated changes will be made. If you have
changes, please send them to me before mid-March.

Federal Junior   Agencies within USDA are alloted positions in this program.
Fellowship   Recruitment is from currently graduating high school seniors,
Program   that 1) will be in a baccalaureate curriculum; 2) be
interested in a Federal career after graduation; 3) be in
the upper 10 percent of their graduating class; 4) have a
demonstrated need for earnings, plus other conditions.
Employment is full-time during summer or other vacation
periods, starting at GS-2 and possibly being eventually up
graded to GS-5. Employment will be at USDA facilities, in
the interest area of the student. For more information,
contact:
    USDA, Office of Personnel
    Room 1078, South Bldg.
    14th & Independence Ave., S.W.
    Washington, DC 20250
    202-447-5625

Richard D. Reynnells
Richard D. Reynnells
Program Leader, Poultry Science

CPSIA information can be obtained
at www.ICGtesting.com
Printed in the USA
BVHW010731211118
533509BV00033BA/5286/P